This Book Belongs To

_____

A Gift From

_____

THE Three Sedonas

by LISA SCHNEBLY HEIDINGER

illustrated by TREVOR V. SWANSON

For Tom: Thank you for Sedona and Rye! — Lisa Schnebly Heidinger

For Jennifer, Connor, and Devon: Thank you for all of your love and support.
Also, Doug Anderson, whose beautiful photographs inspired me.
— Trevor V. Swanson

Trevor Swanson's illustrations were created with oil paint on canvas.
Book design by Billie Jo Bishop

Prepared by the Book Division of *Arizona Highways*® magazine, a monthly
publication of the Arizona Department of Transportation.

Publisher NINA M. LA FRANCE
Managing Editor BOB ALBANO
Associate Editor EVELYN HOWELL
Art Director MARY WINKELMAN VELGOS
Production Director CINDY MACKEY

Printed in Hong Kong.
Library of Congress Catalog Card Number: 99-62976
ISBN 0-916179-97-4

FOREWORD

Dear Reader,

When you learn about something that happened a long time ago, that is history. People in this book became pioneers, and a little bit famous, but they didn't know that would happen.

The way they became a part of history was by doing their best, even when it was hard, and by being brave. That means doing what's right, even if you're afraid.

You don't know it now, but you may be an important part of history someday. The world isn't divided into people who will do famous things and people who won't. You can be a leader, a pioneer, or a hero.

If you're going to be famous, make sure it's for good things. Figure out what ways of helping people make you happy. Always try — and don't give up when you're discouraged.

Write about things that are important to you and about what you want to do. That will be part of your history!

Then, when you are an ancestor, people will be very proud to know about you.

LISA SCHNEBLY HEIDINGER

HI. I GET TO TELL YOU THE STORY OF THREE SEDONAS.
The first Sedona I'll tell you about is me. I live in Arizona. I'm six years old. I have a younger brother, Rye. We play pretend a lot. He likes to be a brave warrior riding a daddy lion, and I like to be a princess riding a magic pony.

The second Sedona I get to tell you about was my great-great-grandmother. People say her name is an Indian word, or it means different things, but the truth is, her mama just made it up. When Sedona was a young woman, she married the man she loved. His name was T.C. Schnebly. They lived a long way from here, in a state called Missouri. Then they became pioneers.

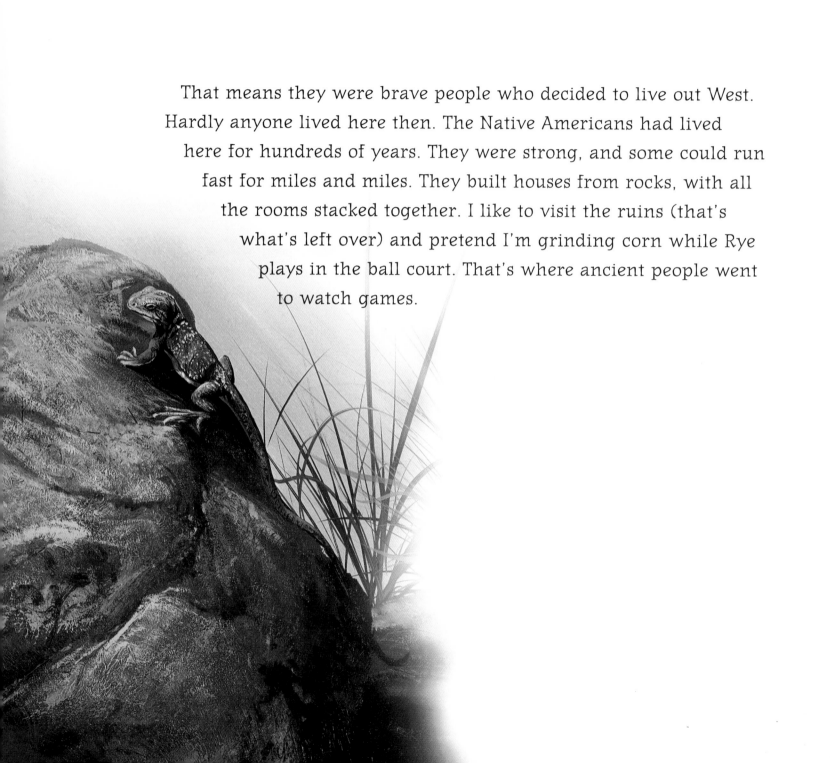

That means they were brave people who decided to live out West. Hardly anyone lived here then. The Native Americans had lived here for hundreds of years. They were strong, and some could run fast for miles and miles. They built houses from rocks, with all the rooms stacked together. I like to visit the ruins (that's what's left over) and pretend I'm grinding corn while Rye plays in the ball court. That's where ancient people went to watch games.

Later on, a few men who hunted bears and other animals
moved around the West, kind of camping out all the time.
Some looked for gold. Some explorers came and made maps.
But mostly the country was pretty empty.

Sedona and T.C. came to a place T.C.'s brother had told him was magical. People thought it was magic, or holy. Maybe because it was so beautiful. There were towers and mountains of rocks that glowed like stone fire, with skies so blue they looked like the ocean. Lots of birds and animals lived there, but it was so quiet you could hear the winds leaping through the tree branches. The place was called Oak Creek Canyon.

When Sedona and T.C. moved to Oak Creek, they built a house. It had an upstairs and a downstairs. So when people came west and wanted to see Oak Creek, they stayed with Sedona and T.C. Their house was turned into a sort of hotel.

Sedona must have been so busy! She had many visitors to feed. In those days you had to cook over a fire, so you had to chop or collect wood. And the red rocks that were so pretty made dust that stained their clothes. So Sedona walked down to the creek to do all the laundry by hand. She had to watch all the time to make sure her little children didn't fall in the creek while they played. She scrubbed the clothes on a washboard, like this one.

T.C. had to go away a lot, selling the apples and vegetables they grew. Up from the canyon, a town called Flagstaff is too cold for people to grow those things. It took four days to get there, so T.C. and some other men built a road up Schnebly Hill. They used big scrapers pulled by horses. You can still drive on Schnebly Hill Road. It's really bumpy! Sedona would ride her horse to take them lunch when they worked.

Once when T.C. was gone, Sedona was with her children in the garden and heard a sort of dry buzzing sound. It was a rattlesnake! He was sitting next to a rock. A snake could kill a child by biting it. Sedona was very brave, which means she was scared but she did something anyway. She grabbed a rake and just hit that snake right on the head and killed it.

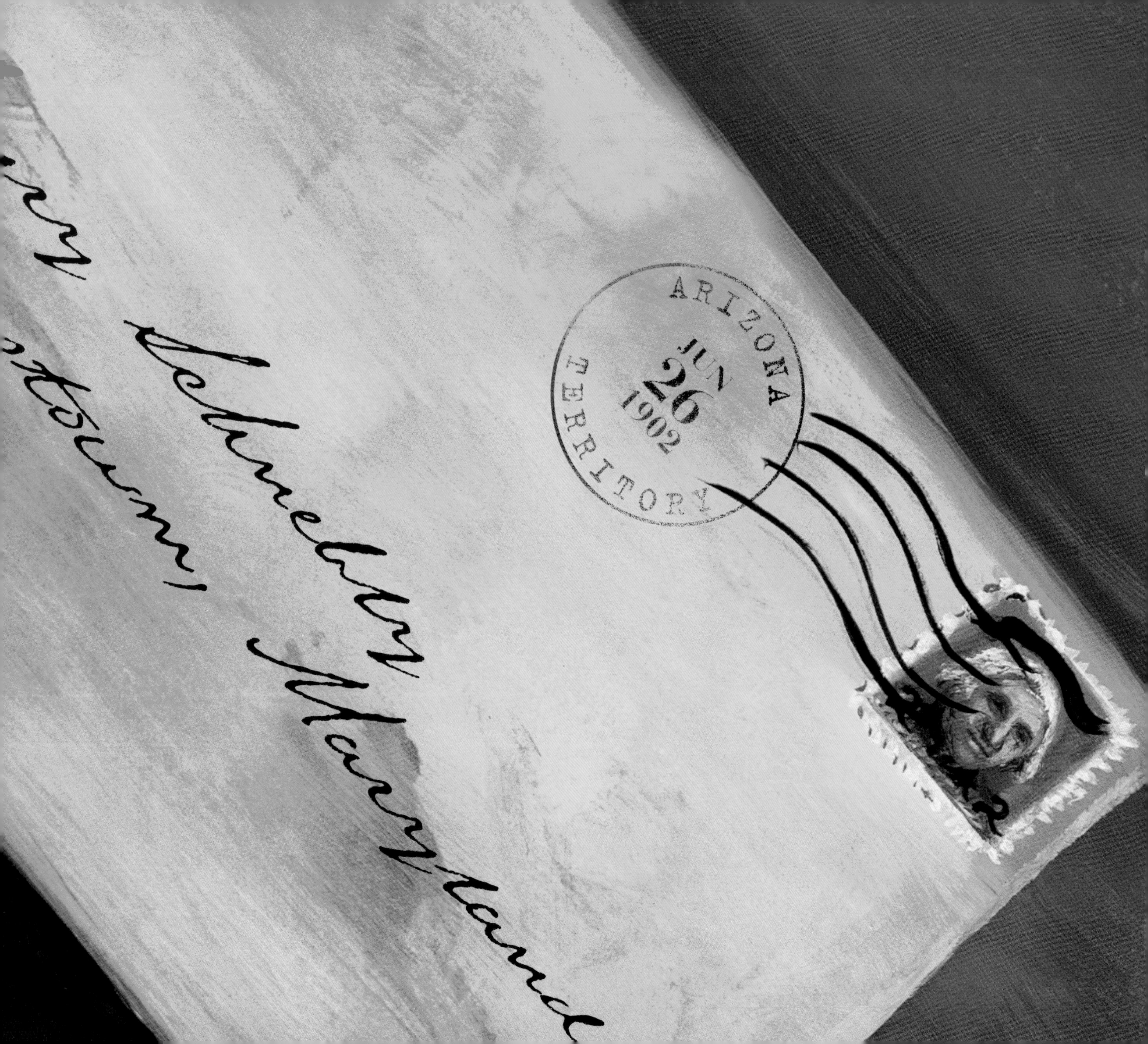
ARIZONA TERRITORY
JUN
26
1902

T.C. wanted to be a mail carrier, but people couldn't get letters in Oak Creek because they didn't have a town. They needed to live in a town with a name so someone could write it on an envelope and the letter could be delivered.

T.C.'s brother said, "Let's name it after Dona." That was Sedona's nickname. T.C. thought that was a great idea. I bet Sedona was embarrassed, and it probably made her feel very proud.

So this is the third Sedona. It's the town T.C. named after my great-great-grandmother. She died a long time ago, so I bet she wouldn't recognize it if she visited now! Hundreds of families live here, instead of just a few. And instead of her apple orchards, there are stores and places to look at paintings, called galleries. Lots of artists live here because it's still so pretty. I like to go to Tlaquepaque and see the fountain and the chapel.

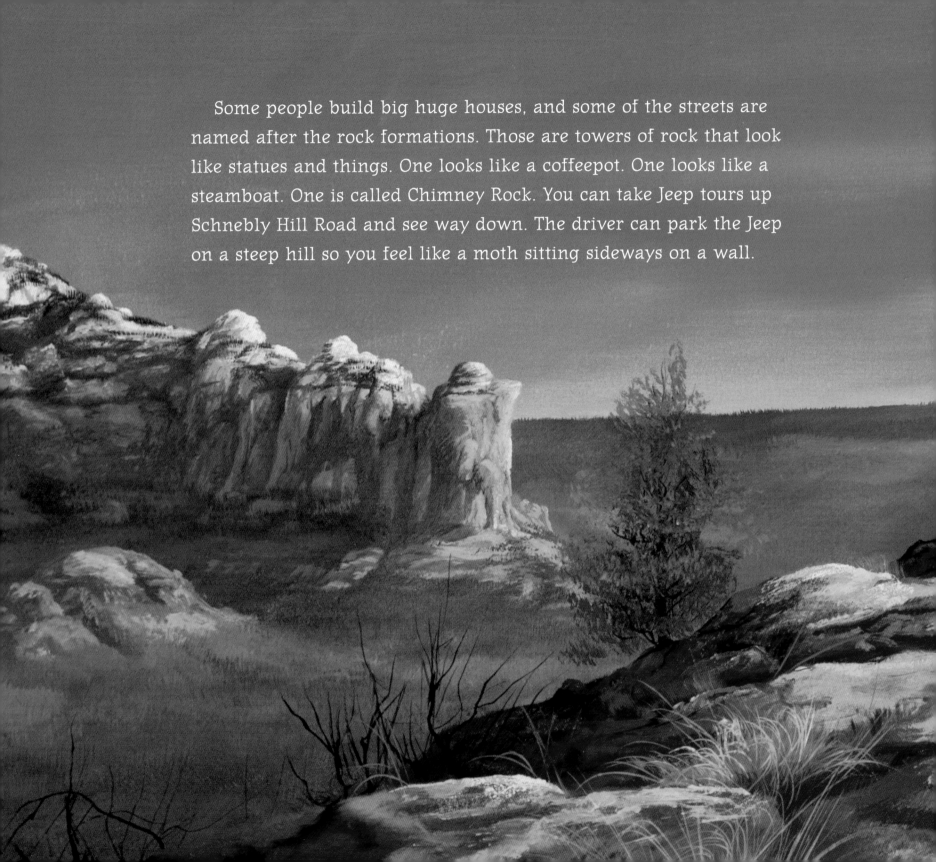

Some people build big huge houses, and some of the streets are named after the rock formations. Those are towers of rock that look like statues and things. One looks like a coffeepot. One looks like a steamboat. One is called Chimney Rock. You can take Jeep tours up Schnebly Hill Road and see way down. The driver can park the Jeep on a steep hill so you feel like a moth sitting sideways on a wall.

On the land where Sedona's house used to be, there's a resort called Los Abrigados. A resort is an elegant hotel. The chimney from Sedona's house is still here. It's part of a little home called Stone House. The resort kept it. I thought that was nice.

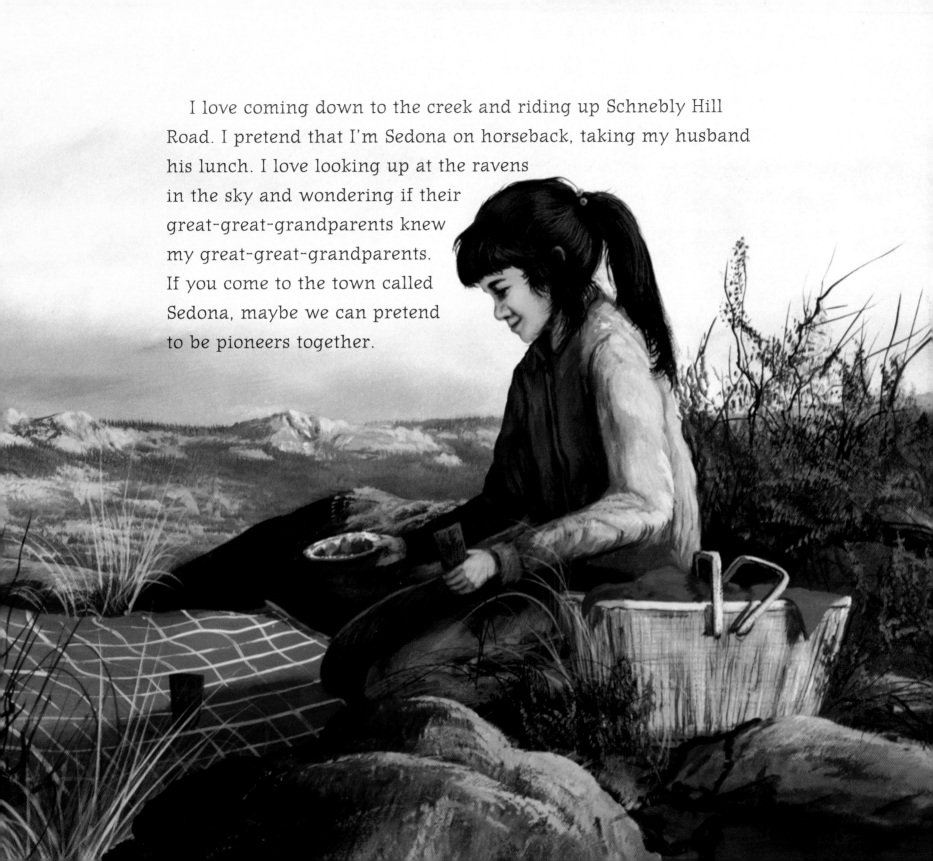

I love coming down to the creek and riding up Schnebly Hill
Road. I pretend that I'm Sedona on horseback, taking my husband
his lunch. I love looking up at the ravens
in the sky and wondering if their
great-great-grandparents knew
my great-great-grandparents.
If you come to the town called
Sedona, maybe we can pretend
to be pioneers together.

LISA SCHNEBLY HEIDINGER has been telling stories about Arizona, her native state, most of her adult life — in community newspapers, editorial columns, and magazines and as a television reporter. She lives with her husband, Tom; children, Sedona Lee and Rye Schnebly; and dog, Happy Jack. All share her passion for "going in the car." Her next project is a biography about her pioneering great-grandmother, Sedona Schnebly.

Photos © Larry Lindahl

TREVOR V. SWANSON is an Arizona artist best known for his beautiful wildlife paintings. This book marks Trevor's first endeavor in the field of children's books and has been a great opportunity for him to paint the incredible scenery in and around Sedona. He lives in Phoenix with his wife, Jennifer, and two children, Connor and Devon.